Daytime Astronomy
PAUL GRATTAN

salmonpoetry

Published in 2011 by
Salmon Poetry
Cliffs of Moher, County Clare, Ireland
Website: www.salmonpoetry.com
Email: info@salmonpoetry.com

Copyright © Paul Grattan, 2011

ISBN 978-1-907056-76-5

All rights reserved. No part of this publication may be reproduced or transmitted in any form or by any means, electronic or mechanical, including photography, recording, or any information storage or retrieval system, without permission in writing from the publisher. The book is sold subject to the condition that it shall not, by way of trade or otherwise, be lent, resold or otherwise circulated without the publisher's prior consent in any form of binding or cover other than that in which it is published and without a similar condition, including this condition, being imposed on the subsequent purchaser.

COVER IMAGE: *'Untitled', Oil on board, 27in x 22in by Cormac Healy –*
www.cormachealy.com
COVER DESIGN: *Siobhán Hutson*
PRINTED IN IRELAND

Salmon Poetry receives financial support from The Arts Council

i.m. Mairtín Crawford

Acknowledgements

Acknowledgements are due to the editors of the following publications:

Ars Poetica Anthology 2006 (Slovakia); *Cyphers*; *Poetry Ireland Review*; *Landing Places: Immigrant Poets in Ireland* (Dedalus Press); *When People are Amazed to See the Trees* was commissioned by Bord Scannán na hÉireann/the Irish Film Board for the Short Shorts Film, *Maze*, directed by Hugh McGrory and read by Adrian Dunbar. Special thanks are due to the Arts Council of Northern Ireland for an Arts Award in 2008 that kept me from bedlam; Chris Kelly and Joseph Woods who remain, hard but fayre.

Contents

Carvery Country	13
A Cauld House	14
Devil's Purse	15
Stars and other Toys	19
At Lurgan	21
Sick Child, after Metsu	22
Panic, for the Original Lager Lovelies	23
Bás in Erin	25
Falls	27
In Imitation of Eugenio Montale's, *Previsioni*	29
Erne	30
Strings	31
Mushroom Eaters	33
Arbat Prestige	35
Der Schwere Panzer	36
An Orthodontic Survey of Moscow from a Bar Window	37
Waking to Sochi	39
Pushkin in Shanghai	40
Private Lives	41
Daytime Astronomy	42
The Ship Inn	43
A Bit of a Sketch	45

The Blessing of the Animals	47
When People Are Amazed To See The Trees	52
Discovery	54
Schrödinger's Bap	56
Everyone Here is Charming	58
Plenary Pieces	59
Climbing the Jung Frau	63
The Suffering General	64
Ankles	65
Man wi a Melodeon	67
The Modern Scot Invokes a Bust of Walter Raleigh	68
Saddling	69
Fishamble	70
On the Question of Discipline for One Who Won't Wear Rubber	71
Cavalry of Sin	72
Velázquez in the Iveagh Gardens	73
Following Sea	74
Varnishing Days	75
An Even Devotion	76
About the Author	79

We have all been processed on Procrustean beds.
R. D. LAING, *The Politics of Experience*

Ten properties of an object, according to Leonardo: light and dark, colour and substance, form and position, distance and nearness, movement and stillness.
ROBERT BRESSON, *Notes on The Cinematographer*

I saw approch, agayn the orient sky,
A saill, als quhite as blossum upon spray,
Wyth merse of gold, brycht as the stern of day,
WILLIAM DUNBAR, 'The Goldyn Targe'

Carvery Country
for Matty

What makes this country free
is the butterflies plamossing

the vestiges of a breeze
at some stop that's not for changing

of the gauges, herald-mothing
the heartland. I will never sit

comfortably with the Fianna,
removed from this village life

Mutt and Jeff to my people's song,
a shift in skies that makes me

brilliantly upset. Too aloof
for translation, I'll be an under-

stander, midget-wrangler, curly-
bap-straightner, or the sign reading

you have now left Carvery Country.

A Cauld House
for Matthew Ryan Donovan

Early houses had just one room
in which everyone ate and wept

later kips were carved up
into their separate fictions

a red room for the Provider
a wing for the women to grieve

remains of a coup found in Stong
Iceland, mimicked this micrology

a dairy where the dead made cheese
bitter, a lounge for enemies

holes ripped in the breast–
summer shewed smoke away

so rarely the heart became swollen
a reeking lum, licht tae the world.

Devil's Purse
for Maire Frances

In 1629 Valentine Payne wrote the Earl of Kildare that he had built
a Quay at Strangford, *"where there was none before. The biggest shippe
that the King hathe, may lay her side beside it."*

i. Cuan

It was an Ards Peninsula town –
the strong fiord some Viking named

after a season's rapine, stars
countable, attuned to the huffings

of a kelp-quilted lough, a Cheyne-
Stokes breathing for lost Londonderrys

and Castlewards, the last December
of ourselves alone.

ii. Walter's rock

UP DOWN the rock sings, out past Killyleagh
past plumes of smoke an abused chip-pan painted

sky-high,
         ay but they were home-made chips boy

and by the water where we wheel our first and only daughter
swaddled up rightly in her granny's coy, clotted Ulster-

Scots, my heid loups in an accent muted by this bay
                  thrawn as a box of crabs.

iii. The Portaferry Stane

Babs will tell you, Babs who has brought Dalmatians,
tomato and scrumpy chutney, with auld decency will tell you

polluted by drink on Stephen's Day we are not. We have taken
the ecstasy of jingle bells on bird-black beaches to the point

where arguments whip atomies of soot into the Jacobean keep
of the Demesne. And the bonny moorhen is hooked, half-minded

to quit the Narrows definitely this year, this sack-clothed January;
while a boy from the Markets bobs and is lost to his Da', waist-

deep in briny grief and the keening of Mass Cards, who is to say
will not bring comfort, cold or cod, to a coffin's bass relief.

iv. The Corner Boy's Gift for Bifurcation

On Windmill Hill three craws survey a road still ca'd a brae
in Greba, until the world is filled with cawing thaumaturgy. Christ

if ever I said I could murder a crow, forgive me. Mind, yon time
in Carrowdore we parked our Southern plate under their arch

to ask directions for the Kirk. Lively we counted coppers
for ten Purple, not to speak of the Fat Frog, while Louis moldered

in his grave and hard men with mullets, *aye ready*, took their bevy
outside, misreading Kildare for Kerry, keeping the Kingdom true.

v. Afore ye go

We shot the craw, loving the crush of noses against windshield.
At Ardkeen you folded white roses in childhood pockets, pinching

the cold mantle's cheek for old times sake. The Cur passed us
on the Ballybeen Express, a belly on him like a poisoned pup, eyes

peeled shut, doing seventy in a bone-shook Ulsterbus. Poets
are liars right enough, but what would the Gods make of the Irish

at the beginning or gable end of the Estate, *lámh dearg abú*
the stone throwers fate unbreakable, moving a school girl to tears.

vi. Eurydice

Darby and Joan, in the bleached Formica
of their new kitchen. Six bells, eye water spilt

upon the table. She is gone daft watching
her weans pitch and toss beyond the versed out

town, first Liverpool then Dublin. *Fender Park 'll
dae me love* is how the all clear sounds

fae Scrabo Tower tae Cowey's Wells,
as green grows the grass below the gantries oh.

vii. Orpheus

Blair Mayne was a hula-maiden for a Magus so,
his long range desert sass cast in grass-skirted, pelvic-

thrust for the Millenium. *We give artists grants to imagine
war heroes in leafy bowers*, the Jolly Judge explodes. Fu'

Orpheus chaps, has taken his punishment for house-
breaking, can be forgiven but not forgotten for turning

his back on her long fair hair, on My Lady's Road,
sacking a theory of strings for the patter of Powers.

viii. Clough

Small towns have long memories jegs in your craw, rattles
past Clough and something Pop says doesn't bare thinking.

A body in a stour, standing closer than a father should
in the school returning gloom, stoops to hood some wee lad.

Inequities of pottery, wild celery, motte and bailey, a slue
of tin-white cement sacks, old enough to be grist, now laid

to rest with the best mutant Ards statistics. *Living here
you'd kill me*, you protest, putting your foot down, *pack it in.*

ix. The Decommissioning of the Boats

Committed to mud and memory, we've had our fill
of holly on the Mastheads. *Transcend, Laharoi, Advantage,*

thon auld licht lighted up like a pagan Longship. War
whole, shivering timbers tarred with the same brush

that beached the *Corner Boy*, burnt prows and bulldozed
sprits fae Ardglass, Portavogie; black-coated workers,

game's a bogie. For decommissioned berth, take this touch-
tank; nursehound, skate, ray, play empty pursed beside us.

Stars and Other Toys
for Lara

Without having ever seen it, she sleeps
like Bacon's Pope, innocent in the deposed

King-size duvet, between us
and the rest we so dolorously covet.

~

*Whoever would Adam & Eve it,
her auld lad is all of a jock.*

*The post partum grip of a mason,
a gingery nugget on top.*

~

Suppose that on some quantum front
there is some want or anti-want

or *bursa*, employed to wet-nurse
bars away a certain February. Canopic

jars are yours, fly-cemeteries,
baps floury with all the condiments

the full Irish can stomach, where even
a jaundiced nose won't run

forever. Slow motion grace,
stars and other toys

what Paradise is opened by your face.

~

Through Pig Town, Love Lane, Walsh's,
past the tarts, we ride the chicken-

chaser through the bats to the Rotunda –
Romania, Nigeria, Drumcondra, congrats.

~

Silver for the babbie born in spring,
your given name's all Greek to me

Larissa, Neptune's fifth satellite. Hats
scarves and banners fill me, fu'

tae the gunnels wi shy beauty, I think.
You look like a rice cake in orbit, Heuston

far away trains passing by –

At Lurgan

So then because thou art lukewarm, and neither cold nor hot,
I will spue thee out of my mouth

                                                      Rev. 3:16

I thought at Lurgan we had found our European home –
yet how little shoulders shrug for the tenderness of page

all those good or bad intentions with which
ordinary looks are paved and how much we sink

in those few fields submerged a mile or so outside
a lion's den from which no tracks return. Mad Pup

lies wounded Sir, not dead but does any of this hold
water? A rictus of the hood whose fink is loyalty

yon Blue Nun of the damned. What has mythology
to do with being wrong? In the Mirror let it be read

Da' built his pecs like Oppenheimer built his bomb –
at night, in kinky black and white, for want of devastation.

Mad bitches on the platform flirt to polished chrome
by so much vaunted, damp and massive hardness.

These are my daughters and my daughter's age –
blink and be born again, beyond compassion.

Sick Child, after Metsu

Ut pictura, poesis,
    HORACE

Scittery, scattery do you lie, after a winter's teat,
in neat American Freedom baby-grow, our baby

Lenin lookey-likey. To make words up, love –
under the arbour that hangs on the hill, *Mons Palatinus*

Sorrento's chip, rent town of crane and cappuccino,
all touching pressure, given to lip, feathered by breath

uttered by mouth, held in the ear, set down with fingers,
still to the eye you inhabit more than one wing

peasant scenes and faces, canvases creatured
by Turner's seascapes, interiors and prisons, taverns

Horace never knew. Teething on raw enchantment,
you are the spit of Metsu's sick child, forcefully drawn

listlessly tender, an untouched earthenware bowl
of pap, bare beside a brownish ankle.

Panic, for the Original Lager Lovelies

Have you guessed you yourself would not continue?
Have you dreaded these earth beetles?
    WALT WHITMAN, *To Think of Time*

i. Maid of the Loch

Like insects on the surface of the water, this whirligig
is killing us; we need arms, a word that figures often

in our *gotterdammerunging* round the houses, calling-
on songs, a cankerfret of charms, to forget Ann

the founding bird of the red & yellow can – mooning
for steamers on the bonny banks, willowy, gloomy tans

dying their Northern roots – June's gypsy dress, Norma
with a rose, Trish on the cliffs, on the Glen road, in the ice-

cool 500ml version, nothing less will do. Janis sits pretty,
crimped neck in three piece steel and ring pull, a kind

but Northern kitsch that mingles succour, with a seven
or seventy-five year itch. Beat the wife at home, war clouds

over Drimnagh, we swallow mothers' pride, outsiders
of Pan; enough to go a roving, for whom should we disarm?

ii. Ridged Lands

Here are people lost in space
in the Hippocratic sense, advancing low lives

among mould and vegetation, sunk climate
of blood groups on pavement, crimson hair-lip

over gloss supposedly lamenting the loss
of buried pleasure, lip-stick blotted on bills

like ringworm, coz, kiss & tell, you're worth it,
that's why human beings conceal, almost

all of it, features of habit. *Sub specie
aeternitatis*, pure acting the maggot in Crumlin

might be mistaken for a shell-suited take on
The Taking of Christ – somewhere I love you

more than spunking wages at the weekend.
We split a twelve-ounce can, to drown our drumlin.

Bás in Erin
for Joseph & Sarah, June 14th 2003

When you are tired and overhung with drink
consider the rashers, pink and portly in Portumna,

DJ sacking his decks for the ride ahead
in Galway. Remember Pounder, 1916 as street fight

or put another way, *stramash* and all that shite
about Hurling. Pull me a church bell forever

singing in some Midlands town, with nothing
bar hedgerows and heavy children passing

where cricket shall be played to the tap of leather
on willow or stranger still, Bowie beating his Lam-

beg, *auf Deutschland*. We drink and we drink
though we never recover the hour on the hill

of Slievemore village, relics of conacre drifting Asia-
wards to Paddies, as the pause in pips dialled out

past Capricorn quickens the blood, sharpens the horn –
typical, she never has it on, he never hears it anyway.

~

In Keem bay already a dolphin is decomposing
into verse, while *Mir* dandles heavenwards. Glean

if you will, Great Heads you have known – some dote
on French splashed glazes, thumbed and sagging

bases of English medieval jugs and faces. Others
lacking alterity, lurk in the annals of Ship Street

like lovers on a Grecian Urn, touch but never kiss;
so make this day a harvest home, fleshed

and cut from Persimmon, with every stroke of pen
a date-plum, smelling of ampersands; only

a rub of the Ro-co-co to bend your bad ear
inclining, like a left-leaning handle, towards a neck

Burne-Jone's might have stained glass with.

~

You have chosen the hairiest man in Achill
as your bridal sweet, for you are terribly fond
of sleeping. Go

lay your lovely head tonight
in Leiden, Louth or Cashel in Munster;
that all the Woods

may echo, with our wishes ring
a life loved long, a wet mouth
and death in Ireland

a good thing.

Falls
A Trip on the Lagan Toepath, i.m. Mairtín Crawford

Mairtín, *mo chara*, you were the bomb
toting Ginsberg who would not bomb

from Fitzroy to Finaghy, equally beat
on Mars or Broadway. Brutal in a *keiner*

oder alle kinda way, I won't beg you
come back with big sighs – how to lament

(in lines of speed & dregs & diphthongs)
dissent, belief in portents? Mournful comets

        will fly, *Makar*
        up West as night falls.

      ~

Tak our Molly's breasts, ephemera, reluctantly
sequestered, straining a Methody girl's recuscancy

& the rest of us, sadly lacking in classical restraint,
admonished by a site-specific sand culture. Stephen's

Green in bloom, ay, the band stand all perfume
& vague Garda Síochána. Let the red, lettered clay

stay the clouds of your eyes, from every Southern
slight or blurt, triumph & disdain, to batter hearts

& Mars bars, look up the skirt O'Hara nailed, fleshed
into cosmic space dust. Matchmaker, cosmopolite

celestial cook, *mo chara*, the girl from the Ferry
you pulled me, has me a father. As to the sleet of late

witless as it falls on the Black Mountain, on our Irish daughter,
upon the bitter Whin, these are cryptic matins a bird-brain plays.

Partly you loved the sot of dreams, itself a departure
lovers sometimes broach; but the essence of delay is parting

not to reproach blossom linger over the brief bloodstream.
Chapel bunged, woman shoulder their world, *oh, too soon.*

~

Neither retreat or advancement makes this day iconic,
palatable, possessed of symmetry. In the City

where you're planted it's cold beyond a joke. Overhead
skates Mercury turned to lead, brandy-wine to syrup.

Limp oak imputes with an itch of rope burning neck-
wards. Normally, you would never be seen dead

in yon beige hue & and cry. Pity for words, a foiled rose
greets graveside, you leave us restless, why, Rocket?

Pulling boats in the back bar of Lavery's Gin Palace,
whispering of stars. Last night's dry boke, beloved

Bonaparte, maintaining, *the duty of the avant garde
is to manoeuvre.* Broken is the soil, the bed unmade

token ventilator hovers breath in. Fall guy, Mariner, *mo
chara* it's late & slowly, blackbirds bait about your forehead.

In Imitation of Eugenio Montale's, *Previsioni*
for Marco Sonzogni

                Body-swerve in the garden
hanging, by the way, to duck

                the soft tongue of a new lodger,
you speak of poets' birds

created to pad unreadable rooms.
                So it is with me, you murmur.

           Petrified, I manage
remember bullets are blind

            to the target as well as
the trigger finger.

            But we're not in some tin pan alley – *see*
I don't believe you're packing.

Erne

for Dean, on leaving Her Majesty's Service

Away to the lorn
run Rifles at play

tint of fur
hints a water-snake

otters in spay.
Shall we shoot it then

son? Signify
lough as lake

return to do Pinter
blow rams horn

dun winter.

Strings

Ich bin der Welt abhanden gekommen

After the brothers die, my thoughts run
from Mahler's *Kindertotenleider*, beyond

the droll of a melodeon, a weeping willow
or acacia, over a brothers' grave, towards

first flute, looking backwards in its own way
to loving dreams of past sonorities, recalling

perhaps the slightly forced adoption of a jolly
public face, set from a different angle. Tears

broil the starry heaven, vaulting enough
to remain in mind, tam-tam, celesta, harp

English horn, long after tumultuous scherzo's
decline, fearfully strained as they strive

to sustain bare unearthly harmonies
on the lips of Hapsburg weans.

~

Feeling new strings, it must be the *jings*
in *crivens* moves me unerringly towards Librium

to unstop my mouth, perform libration of the moon
dissolve in the impetuous, fag ash parallels

of Rückert's loss, embracing and taming them
yet the world   *wetter*   inhabits, insists normality

be skewed as a bi-polar disorder played on the spoons
in the tart gin'n'tonic D Major, the mordant half-bar

dislocation of a lover's phonic shift, tumbling coot-
wards, a cap of great Scotch mist, topped by a scum

of curls. Beyond this and beyond this again, the fine
line between love archly lowers the pine-stripped tots

six or so feet under their allotted plot. Time to waltz
words, just enough pneumatic drafts'manship to puff

fitfully, construct a foxes paw, bowler-hatted trifles
stitched between floating ribs, to claw or stifle absence

workaday duns, dirtied bibs and fakes, I frankly do
not know what you call the finale – on hearing Grand Master

fist the Violinist, *you think I fash about your wretched fiddle
when the spirit shakes* – hap long the bower fresh to the hour

supple and night-full, ripe until dawn, unravelling rooms,
an empty chest, in this weather, in this gale they rest

lued, aye in their mammy's house, an toom kist.

Mushroom Eaters
for Elena & Anton Kononenko

i. K 56

While we are sorting out the oysters
from the drowned, you call to mind

each one, where you found them,
how they first frowned and grew

beneath this birch, that pine, *beryoza,
bor*. Crimson-kissed, their shadows

flavour where the dark firs drift
before the gulf of Finland. They hunt

no longer on the forest meadow.
Tanyusha thins, her dress spilled red

with white secluded beauty spots
arousing a quiet convexity in men

who believe in Lenin
in the legend, in the rain

who stoop to pick boletus
ignore the missus, miss the train.

ii. *I am writing blindly*

Shoeless Anton spins on one foot
(wee boy, white hood, red cap)

into the forest empty he swims
out of the forest full to brim

Antoshka, Antoshka
fill up your basket

with a sweet overflowing
mushroomy, bready sound.

Raw eater of Lenten meats
don't leave us in the ground

at the mercy of Pagans
surrounded by Fly-killers.

iii. News from Vidyayevo

No agarics were taken.
All the sea pockets

for her dinner table,
tawny *edulis,* brown *scaber*

red *aurantiacus,*
a few close mates

and a mariner's dumb bell
audible for days.

iv. K 141

My brothers' graves are there,
the mushroom eaters taught.

Zakuski from your dacha,
plumbs from your father's plot.

Arbat Prestige

It makes it worse
everyday to know

they are here
in her Louis Vuitton

purse, lip-stick, eye
shadow by Armani

~

too dolled up
for the old *muzhik*

girl let them glow
as small joys

blush cheeks with beet-
root, nature's beauty

~

she's lost control
of her make up

buys what he likes
from Brown Thomas

throes Irish life
the odd bone

life's hard here
people tire like children.

Der Schwere Panzer
for Ute Nissen

Kinski rasps Villon with a tart
so Black Forest you could split trees

between syllables, love wallpeckers, even
wired to his strawberry mouth.

Give me the power to limp on before
the heavy armour shoves, for nails to be ripped

from fingertips, inflamed by an Ostalgie
stiffened by thug elections. What if

she is necking your schnaps with sok
thieved from more pleasing thoughts –

We stall the ball outside Tsarskoye
Selo. Yuri, Vova, Marienka – the fall

when it comes is swift; *Die Mauer*
muss weg T-shirts & *Hermitage* mugs.

An Orthodontic Survey of Moscow from a Bar Window

for Macdara, on his Sixtieth Birthday

> *As Maeterlink observed, 'you can do everything with bayonets except sit on them'.*
> ALDOUS HUXLEY, *The Ultimate Revolution*

It's like the poor man's Nutcracker in here –
we open up with the justification for Hiroshima

Bar Man from Mali, free-pouring edicts
of an early house, Moscow mulling into snow

outside the world's biggest folly.   Spook
from Virginia's never heard of Cavan – *Working*

together, the unquiet American yawls, *the women
of Tomsk can get better prices for their handsome assets*

even when harvests are bad.   Like priests of our state
we black out – compensation to the clergy

on the night in day shift –   dark pools of spit work
lending boiled, sweet faces a brassy, candlelit repose.

★

*Aint nothin
orthodox in sadness at six bells, howlin for drink*

*while the curs of the Kremlin larrup their balls
before barking up the wrong tree.*

Huế, Khe Sahn, Dien Bien Phu, broken teeth
on vodka roam the rooms and suites of the Rossiya.

★

*An army
of twenty tongues, all business, at Borosova
that November, attempting to ford the Berezina*

*Bony found the bridge had been destroyed. His boys
erected trestles from the living lumber of a village*

*pontooned, burning the bends behind. All ashen-
faced laundry, bundles of bed-linen, soaps and howls*

*hand-creaming the centuries, hanging apart from men,
swinging to and frau, I have tried to remember those toiletries*

*and robes among the blocked, to concentrate my mind
on the next village but who will lead us to the gates of Vilnus?*

*Carry on up the chimney, brazen as Zhukov on his steed,
a good-natured dog, friendly to my jews, I have tried to retain*

*the you and me of a chair, a rock, a hammer, a girl I refrain
engaging – the only way to drink is to endure.*

★

Three days, ay, slowly bleeding the elephant dry
and the nights are fair drawing in, without treading

or tasting black sea water; behind free *champanska* glasses,
moulded on the well-fired baps of Josephine, Spook

is a rabbit lamped, knocking back *piva* under his sable –
sleep faster comrade, as the oul' alarm clock rings

a last blast of The Weary Provo, before the diaspora of home
disappears him to Sochi, gabled with black state cars

still in love with dentists for their wide horizons.

Waking to Sochi

An arcade project to miss, foul
feathery surds, a playground

of black sea bumpkins, expunctions
smudging the sky line. Now

will I credit cognac to rekindle
in me candles – votive, Pascal, party

the kind gone AWOL in power cuts,
untouched in their pelts of sly dust

marshaled top to toe with thoughts
of going to be consumed. How

I hoped to be accurate to the world
like Gurov in Oreanda, the felt

texture of fingerprints, the high
water mark of private ruin. How

I loved you so much it hurt to piss.

Pushkin in Shanghai

Pushkin in the '30's must have looked a sight –
this stone guest, vagrant, occidental, no mute

swan, nosing his way through Pudong, less cob's
oak-orange plated bill, migrating true West

to proletarian smog, than Lycium fruit,
calyx ruptured by the swollen belly, fragrant

exile, martial bust of Autumn's author. Party
girl, ripe wolfberries in charcoal suit, lingers

for her man or bus, both or neither. Time waits
heavier than bronze as manually conditioned hands

begin the universal gesture of the frozen. Leaves
fill the measure of her gait. He pockets fingers.

Private Lives

I stoop   to feel the dropped drip of a tap
above drawn water, the heart-tick

of a clock before fumbling in flexi-time
for work, your wee bump waxing lyrical

to ventricle, aorta, an amniotic paddling pool
in someone else's mortgage, the warm

swoop of your back's bareness, light as a bag
of cans in Stoneybatter. What wrecks

my buzz tonight in New Heaven & Earth,
in all fairness, a last but Hundred Pipers fling

try Scottish Leader, aye for the long bed of death?
I have less luggage than cowards bring

for short time in the Peace Hotel. Old school
sweetie, one simply doesn't mention baggage.

Daytime Astronomy
for Peter Doig

In which a young man lies on his back
staring up at the sky. He seems to be home

but seven sisters tongues are tied, slack
with fuss while others, plough and sow

there are sounds below in the grass, horrible
pusstular excrescences and the weather all-wrong

perhaps he has more portentous limits
in mind, vowing to work the land, outflows

of rock porridge, sacral bone, daytime astronomy
cry it, ritual clusters mulched by millet.

Little by little he is transformed, stilled
or occupied by light, lying outside a barn

smacked or hypnotized by Pleiades; momently
halted, bounded by this solitude of loan –

The Ship Inn

i.m. *James Simmons & Edwin Morgan*

> *Very deep is the well of the past. Should we not call it bottomless?*
>
> THOMAS MANN, *The Tales of Jacob*

1.

And there were woods of yew to hang from,
weirs in Drymmen to drown sorrows,
orchards to ripen recoil from a twelve-gauge

to the chin, quarries culled from green belts
with losses cut to fit, where Mull's Mire conspired
to suck Adidas Kicks from unctuous ankles,

Monkey Puzzle boughs to dreep and cast
down kernels on Fifth Year's Roman Prefect,
chucked the back of six, twisted on snakebite.

2.

Little has changed since our Passion –
gangs of youth, Tiki, Cumbie, Valley,
even the Young Team have moved upwards

and on to bottomry, the Ship Inn. Spital's crew
let down their bruised arms and tins of Brasso
to *laager* in Magaluf, in the Boozers of ex-Celts

buried, like real Scots who read the Record
from back to front, shocked, stunned, stravaiged
by coupons of truth and *Welt* engorging envy.

3.

May Mungo's great victim-soul complexion
gorgonize & gown in equal, quarter gill measure –
grace-stroke of my heart, we parted gracelessly

nine lives ago for Antrim's cursive rills, kismet
wrested from the muck of land-rails, golden orioles,
the open bath robe of the gray, bearded crooner.

Auld John of Gaunt, who stole your scone,
left land-sick for the Mull & Paps of Jura? Gull-
white Knight, kiln for cooling hopes, erotic schooner.

4.

Like jujubes to an elephant, I swally Granny Blacks,
musked with oul' dolls well past closing. 50p's on teeth,
part-owned, muscle in on cockles, whelks, vinegar-honed

fingers, havering for yon red breast in apron of middle years
to lay her pickled eggs on the low table. The brain mocket
with a confusion of night songs is rowing back again –

Hazel, quare hacket, fish-hooks I can hang my nips on,
ring of a bell maybe, afore the cleft pebble of her lip
skirls the stairs and scalds, *finish up yir gless n go.*

A Bit of a Sketch

i. Plumbs
for Eoghan McGrath

Beneath the swallowed steps of Via Merulana
she gives me back my hand. If indeed she is a man

she is a man's man for a' that, and all the gods
would stand were I to fetch Amaro for her glass.

She's got Dickey Davies eyes – I feel them sketch
your groove in mincing black, slack and lutulent

as Rio – spooning up her dress to party out of here
in plumes of quince and brass. All fingers

and thumbs, I want to stress, *we're back on the sauce,
we've had the all clear.* Yon pimp is on to plumbs.

ii. Pages
for Raymond Gerard Gunning

In the Bibliothèque Nationale, Phnom Penh,
fans circulate the pages of each Symbolist

in the ken of yellow, crimping walls. No one
reads French here anymore. No one hears

Samuel Barber's adagio for strings, cool, kindle,
winnow a basket of agitated air on broken spines

disorient, turn from the East, decline the tableaux
of drunken tractors reared above your father's gate.

No one minds Corbière throwing shapes –
Finger me, dust wakes. Away, I'll take my own bent.

iii. Making Strange
for Julie, who left her tights and dress in Michael's room.

Say you approach her at a bus stop murdering
thou still unravished bride of quietness

she is aware first of the homespun, skelly-eyed
balaclava, the thick, cleated sole of native brogue

rogue short snub puffing it's pigeon-chested
stock beneath white Dunnes Stores bottoms

the barely organised violence, an Aran-
sweatered beak awash in ignorance and rush-

hour static from Craigavon. *Catch yourself on
wee lad.* Redress the suitor's navel and jog on.

iv. The Cat's Pajamas
for Hugh McGrory

It's not the devil on the world's wall vexes him
or whether or not *trouts will be shot* — he has dry-

flied with the men of violence. It's not the Canon,
deceased, morbidly obese, in his seventies

who led a predatory life, didn't want for his deserts
just and good enough for him. What gets his goat

is the note of delay the glass sounds
on the tiled floor of the Telstar as it hits rock bottom

the diagonal motion of sarcoptic swarms,
the porcine/dasein-ness of it all. The cat's pajamas.

The Blessing of the Animals
for Oliver Lyons

> *To discover the NEW WORLD: that there is something there: what it has done to us, its quality, its weight, its prophets, its — horrible temper.*
>
> WILLIAM CARLOS WILLIAMS, *In the American Grain*

I am beginning to list
Mater Cara —

I am broom to my savior
I am no one in particular

I am not a sniper, butcher
parachute maker

I am surly John the Divine
is closed. I am trying to decline

go knacker drinking
by Grant's tomb

near the White Horse, the Cedar
the Henry Street Ale House

I ask for something to eat
a widow's memory

from someone who looks like
Séan the Egyptian

I cannot live besotted
with the village idiot

I cough a lot (sinus?) so
I don't give head

finding the World
Trade Centre ticketed

stot to Battery Park instead
bluter red diesel

off the Staten Island Ferry
as if I were Mindy's Mork

& stormy petrel
do my nesting

in a hoof of sparkling bog water
by the Flat Iron

where mangoes on the sidewalk
split like road-kills

I love myself the drumlins in New York.

~

In Brooklyn once
in her dislocation

she opened the gas-tap
in praise of him.

~

The Hardy Boys restoring
Ur that spring of the gamin

& in the Diner on Houston
he is urging the Grand Army

of the Republic towards
the time of their lives

the grape mildew
of her next set of questions

onion bagel sweetness
curt the cheque.

~

Daybreak boozes slovenly
reforms my bed
slurs mind to office

I want to be sure to reach you

purrs a green light
drunks fear
stirs a hornet in the room

yellowing lobster in the cauldron

nothing on the box
sox cut into corners
and spat out lame

the allegorical figure of Nineveh

strictly pelagic
as if the world was your oyster
& where would you be going

oh cup-bearer, pot-boy

Ganymede to Jupiter
& what would you be doing
with your arse in two halves

a hole in the middle & no sign of it mending.

~

Now the yoke of mania
bestrides yon Ziggurut

rejoin the rider of our storm
at the edge of some vast Imperium

his sea is a crushed people
& all the birds are feart

gulls, loons and penguins
bide away

mere bodies have arrow slits
instead of hairs

cormorants in crude
make-up

prehistoric with grief
in the infants.

~

The usual turnout is dogs
a great white cloud of Pyrenees

cats, bats, rats, cattle, wild asses
& creeping things

I usually just wing it
about the way beasts comfort

flavor, reduce blood pressure
let the mood of the animals

guide length, something
appropriately Franciscan

& hip
might be ventured

like, *me arse ating chocolate*
for Ma' Carey's chickens

I use the Aaronic blessing
for the two Saint Bernards

sometimes the local dipso
takes a swing.

When People Are Amazed To See The Trees
for Raymond Watson

> *This maze was not divinely built*
> *But is secreted by my guilt.*
> W.H. AUDEN, 'The Maze'

I have dreamed of film making itself
on sills and ledges, dusting down grates

and gill slit peep holes, bearing the ledger
No pay, no tea; as with a great non-virtuoso

pianist not slapping emotion on to keys
but waiting, like a painter's eternally

fresh canvas, it comes, quavers, semi-
quavers, strikes notes that are rigorously

equal, framing with the same eye
and the same hand a rose burst, nuns

a leg of mutton, the M1's muffled exits
put beyond use, mantled with ivy.

I have heard the roar of a shell fall
on deaf ears by shore roads, wind feinting

retreat from heaven held up by ball-cock
and piano-wire for passing motorists.

It left a wild hole in my heart to find
pots free of champ and marrow fat peas

forced patterns of life, beloved of my cells
and cages.   I have stood at the centre of things

above laundered shirts, rolling tobacco
fine as the flaw in a bowl of bright drinking

or the gray over Lisburn; to fling the button
under doors and there be snagged by a look

or throat in tumult or rag order and I see now
not one stranger has been left without loss, lifted

like a roof of huts when they are broken
before my mouth and I greatly fear each hard

back smile, the blanket laughter, the thinnest
beech of every acre.   What can I do but wonder

when people are amazed to see the trees
because their leaves are moving.

Discovery

> *The account of individual eye witnesses, therefore, are of only qualified value, and need to be supplemented by what a synoptic and artificial view reveals.*
> W.G SEBALD, *On The Natural History Of Destruction*

The more we learn of this yoke –
its lost, forgotten shifts, arcana

ion traps & giddily dichotomous
curves of individual fortune

so there is a quality to its frying
that manages to calibrate

the timbre of our fallen world,
liquefied along with other camphor-

rich trash – broken tortoiseshell
spectacles, discarded Xylonite

dentures, silver negatives melted
down to resin for waterproofing

wings, 10,000 paper crocuses
of artificial Alpine bloom

it would be impossible to sniff
had you ever been there

as if the dirtiest maid in Europe
had wound flechettes like stars

around the neck of the Frauenkirche,
Western Electric's cathode ray

outgassing history, occult, electro-
magnetic smash. The more we learn

of this yoke, so oddly clamorous
the more ordinary folk are lifted.

Schrödinger's Bap (a thought experiment)
for Martin Mooney

What makes us look? Posit a lodger's loaf
at your Granny's, watching real films

with real actors like Chuck Norris
& none of your shiny boys. Steady the buffs

a blue beard of cruel, Saturday matinée all-at-
seaness, buried up to the hilt in Consuelo's

Spanish mane, a leap of faith from a ship
of the line, bucking under swash of dimples

to belt full pelt at canon, circle wagons
with pillows, relieve the Alamo, Khartoum

Big Horn, under a burning bush. Fly,
to bundle Old Glory over the gain-line

at Iwo Jima, Midway, Remagen, to do every
boys own bit of it again & then some. So

should one find Manhattan's lady clinging
to her cone, unkempt, atomic, her face

tripping her, mind yon good Germans
played by Michael Cain & Robert Vaughan

James Coburn carting his cross of Iron
to the Ost. Food for thought beyond the local

unique fusion of prussic logic, a canister mystery
of Mayo, Dijon, Red sauce & Brown

the physics of which leave you gagging; what is it
in the act of observation makes such changes?

Bohr, a baguette man, kens Heisenberg dating
toes of his toast soldiers, curling visibly inwards by '42.

Everyone Here is Charming

Skinny is dancing hip-deep among the spangled.
The angelic doctor winged on Carling was never so disarming.

Everyone here is charming, even the two and a half-wits
on the door with matching penal, Indian Ink decrees.

FUCK & AFF paired off, collocated, writ upon
the sirloin side of the lip. The blue bag of the mind

brings guys and dolls to laze on the verandas of the Lagan,
dogging Delta from flagons. An inky brand

on cardboard pictures, *Ireland's Number One Lady*.
Her summer wrap betrays a lack of couth in dusky plastic.

All night this barrage, this Salvation Army bonnet
boat-rocks locked youth to heaven while *luck be a lady*

tonight calms communal jets. He'd sell us his dander
if he could, flag up this walk for Jesus, stand on me.

Plenary Pieces

i. At The Stag Inn

Say what you see — semi-
wet, spasms of coned light

shadowed in twine
cauterising, repetitious

two opposite, frostless
brass horses, effortlessly

nosebagging the unthink-
able. *Do it for United*

a Crombie urges. Tell it
like it is, call a spade

a spade. Get in there
before you lose another.

ii. Dreaming of the Diamond, on the road to Newbliss

Consider the naming of objects in a field.
The diamond latticed pallets patching the gap,
bin bags billowing viscreen over blackthorn

ditches, where the oxen of the sun might come
to mount and masticate, rose-fingered cairns
of pock-marked manna. Newly breached

she takes a size thirteen in stocking feet
and pops the crucial question. *Is that a cream puff
or a meringue?* No, you're right.

iii. Memphis in Cootehill

          Just give me a sign –
like a toad tumbling

       from pool
cued clouds, racked above

the Big House;
      the way

        they wear their ears –
soft lads playing winner

stays on, to the Beast
        of Elvis

at Xmas, or a wife
        sacked in Clones.

We can't go on forever –

relax the head,
      I'll start listening.

iv. Saudade, *for Sally*

        Skulking by the lough
I press you for names of trees

       I can't remember
in my urban blindness.

       Come September,
Ash is the last to give up leaves

        and you in Cypress
leaving the morning room behind

          painting by candle
breasts for water lillies

          knives, forks and fish-gut,
prayers from the Portuguese.

v. No Mad Voyage

I have pulled hundreds of them –
the mortal devil's claw, all jaggy
nettled breath and evanescence

through fields of fainting Dutchmen.
I am not a heroine. Midges are vicious
bastards if you have them cornered.

Two dead rabbits and a blue eye
in two days. The wee one eats
the big one first then stiffens after

wick or poisoned. *Wish you were hares*,
the disillusionment hidden
in things – ruts to sink my fragile vessel

don't perturb me. Deadly nightshade
dips its tyrian purple bells, pressed
into Boyne water. Respect the Gut.

vi. Drumlin Number One

The soup bone draws its life
from those around.

A swallow's rise and dip
of exaltation with the rain

lets fall a snail shell
on the sculpted garden.

Someone came gluttonously
at night, I'd say, to dine

on flank and mutton. Know
everything is put away for winter.

Climbing the Jung Frau

She is losing her marbles in the snow,
the splay of sun upon each still confounded eye

milk thistle birls to nuns in winter
blindness, bare knees vistas, edelweiss and ginger

wine. In Julie Andrews steps we climb the cliff
up to the crofter's table, white as doe-ray-me

or Dover. But this is Largs, the Go-Go-Burn,
midges hoaching round a past I feel

we should belong to. Hard to follow, the trig
point looked up to, golden daffodils uprooted

abraded to distraction, sea punished below,
pure pellucid, throwing it's childlike tantrums

at the Pencil. Such a promontory fulfilled
is where I'll plank your marbles, will you go.

The Suffering General

A pack of gulls that candidly peel off
span after span; posh talk of earth and trees

declining; filth of rivers, wind and lee,
spent fields, black smut of smoke-stacks, aye your cough

have I sent all of them from mind yet trough
this valley hollow, leave daisies rot, see

closer some beauty lie or grassing me
up to heaven for wearing a lion's skin, doff

it for shame and put on nature's costume;
the suffering general and in the family

room where lung cancer man explodes, presume-
ably after a fly puff, lit calmly

it's the small affections of the heart assumed
kill and Christmas; your months mind balmy.

Ankles
for Fran Appritch

Soap
to seal the unspoken
gifts your name
lathers your name

come now, birling light

fingers waxen
drawn
through strange, playful rings
tips melted away

birling light, will you come

let us wash it
let us comb it
let us stretch its skin
towards heaven

pull, birling light, come on

stars on her fingers
stars on her toes
she will have perfume
wherever she goes

birling light, will you sing

butter her up
button her lip
an almond-headed tassie
a knot of lamp shades

come back to us, birling light

mouth your blessings
a bed of dew
a mattress
pure, thin, unyielding

birling light, come ahead

hips cut to candle
half-baked, skint ankles
birling light
count me in.

Man wi a Melodeon
i.m. Hugh McGrath

     A spring returns
his bellows fingers

     swing round the Ards
till well past curfew

     running a fast bark
hame to polkas

     each brass reed marks
the biggest barn dance

     in Ballyward, *Catalpa*
for a song, sounding

     the Pine Tree Riot
Magpie Uniform

     Braid Arrow, to relate
by nature, to belong.

The Modern Scot Invokes a Bust of Walter Raleigh

for Hammy & Dorrie

Ay if ever He were bonny
'twas in Noah's time, one famous

grouse capped day near Hampton Court,
a gun-tipped Man-O'-War bespoke

as pleasant folk of Teddington
who cultivate the whey of beards

and valleys. Hunting & Love by the pale
of the moon are nothing new to Nessie

lost ship mate of this bust, in scales
and horns disporting herself of ports

and wynds and galleys. World was full
of itself then, pawned wedding bands

pensions to choke a dray, Catasta's
brood of tenements and tallies.

Saddling
for Paddy Dillon

They will not run today, the Harriers,
etched in claret, pinks and lime, uncharted

lithographs, behind the times even then,
cantering to post at two or thereabouts.

Under the ink-hearted belly of a mare
a Farrier measures hands, doggy-style

for the paddock, *qua, qua horsiness*.
In *della robbia* white, breeks of a nabob

starched spotless for the day that's in it,
swagger with sporting chance, prepped

to receive the nod, after the Greek Fashion,
saddled between Pomp and Circumstance.

Fishamble

Tadger & Tool, Bud
Dobber & Wang

Wab, Mickey & Lang-Ball
Stonner & Pud

Handel the lad
back of Isolde's

promising something
to make the ladies scream.

On the Question of Discipline for One Who Won't Wear Rubber

Don't dismiss a night in the cupboard –
rubber bagged and melancholy sacked,

the forced march in the park of a stormy
morning, wrists trussed behind the back

in black mackintosh cape and hood,
at the mercy of another Id, in this instance

a gack but whatever the basis of deportment
such as a corset or a snood, until the end

of the continuum is reached, why not
eschew yon sly boots who fondly wears

ball-gag, choke-pear, branks and bids
you *suffer baby*. SUFFER, as the mouse said

mounting the elephant – *bondage
is a great leveller, the harness frees us all.*

Cavalry of Sin

What comes next? Bible John
losing the bap, Salome

waxing lyrical her topaz
snatch, lucky strike

from behind by behemoth
with billhook for fingers

sucker punch to the blind side,
ball-bag tonsured

for a Tetrarch's bint
to lap up like a dummy tit.

Velázquez in the Iveagh Gardens
for Connie

Once he painted fools and cripples,
now he chooses to fix this scene –

barely enough patches of brightness
in the flutes of office workers

to luniform dreams of buskers
next to us, fire eaters, tin-foiled

automatons, tansads folded
on night busses by pre-loved teens;

it's all too much for the maid
and Argus is just a farm boy, capped

to a surplus, Io, morphed
into a cow (one might almost call

her beef Baroque), faded
bodegones on nearly every corner

bodies piled in or stung
by Mercury, some gouger

chalking pavements, truth told
a touch of the traveler in him

crouched, finger on gaff he plans
to plant us with. Cobbled

streets elicit somber, purplish
trams over Venus's bare shoulder

emboldening commuters,
bossed as mirrors in the Alcazar.

Following Sea

For we must first descend if we wish to be raised

Stretching the canvas of her body
to the welter of a café

flecks of eternal weight are being struck
and lost – Naples yellow

Old Holland blue
Hooker's green, Mars violet

mix with rabbit skin glue
talk of a delft susurrus

burn, brook, rill, beck, gill, rivulet

sculling top tables, dancing into air
flared nostrils of seething foam

one vast minute of latitude
stopping a rectilinear heart –

will there be more fucking?

a single sea crossing may suffice
a following sea, parting itself

into a sequence of different mornings –
decaying lotus leaves, dragonflies

dogging over stagnant water
fetching her gaudy, as a dying star

only black ink on rough bamboo
a slow drifting wash – wolf hair

tapered to a fine point, dense and dilute
the sullen *notan* night wears.

Varnishing Days

Some toe-rag has taken time
to labour *Love & Anarchy*

above a Mosque in Shoreditch.
The Sun is God, kids Turner

in his pigments' blindness,
coining London's livery abed.

He has a bit of a gate on him,
bids *shitehawks* sling their hooks

reddening a gasworks,
while whelk weights Emperor

to Elba. From his perspective,
rain, steam, speed is *Opportunity*

a barge disloigned, laburnum
light of varnishing days.

An Even Devotion

i. Integrating the Catastrophe

North o' Down
ahint the Mid-Atlantic claith

of a thrawn lobster town
twa scaldies

coorie in tae a ferm house.
They do not ken that it lies

on a fault line.
There is a massive rummle

followed by an earthquake.
This creates a huge split

in the cran.
They are burd mooth't

nettle-earnest, locals neb
aboon the situation

or catch themselves on
taking it for a dwam

a clean brek
guldered by ice crystals

so they wise up
knocking through walls

a now expanded space
thus integrating the catastrophe.

ii. Krafla Volcanic Fissure Row

Later that day
a huge fissure is sloping away

at the rate of one centimetre
per year of bending bones.

When they hit the Sunrise
she orders sweet and sour

ice crystals melting
his prawns gray.

Author photograph: Chris Kelly

PAUL GRATTAN was born in Glasgow, Scotland, in 1971. He moved to the North of Ireland in 1995, and gained an MA in Creative Writing at the Poets' House/Lancaster University; studying under the late James Simmons. In 2002 *The Edinburgh Review* published his first collection, *The End of Napoleon's Nose*. His work has appeared in several anthologies including: *The New Irish Poets*, ed. Selina Guinness (Bloodaxe 2004); *Magnetic North*, ed. John Brown (Lagan Press 2006); *The New North*, ed. Chris Agee (Wake Forest 2008); *Landing Places*, eds. Eva Bourke & Borbala Farago, (Dedalus 2009). He lives in Belfast and is currently researching a PhD on the work of the Scottish poet and cultural philosopher Kenneth White for the University of Ulster.